let's eat less meat

vegetarian recipes for meat eaters

by oliver boaler

WH⬤LE PUBLISHING

Let's Eat Less Meat

Published by

Whole Publishing

11 Woodland Park, Calne, Wiltshire, SN11 0JX

www.wholepublishing.com

Copyright © Whole Publishing

ISBN 978-0-9934803-0-0

Author: Oliver Boaler
Photographs: Oliver Boaler
Artwork: Oliver Boaler

Printed in Poland

For marketing and sales enquiries: wholepublishing@gmail.com

First edition 2015

50% of the profits from this book go to Orkidstudio, a humanitarian design charity whose focus is to benefit children and communities worldwide through innovative architecture and construction.

to find out more visit
orkidstudio.co.uk

Orkidstudio is a registered Scottish charity - Charity number SC041184

introduction

I wrote this book, not as a vegetarian but as someone who enjoys a roast dinner or a bacon sandwich as much as the next guy. There is however, equally tantalising food without meat, and so many reasons to eat it.

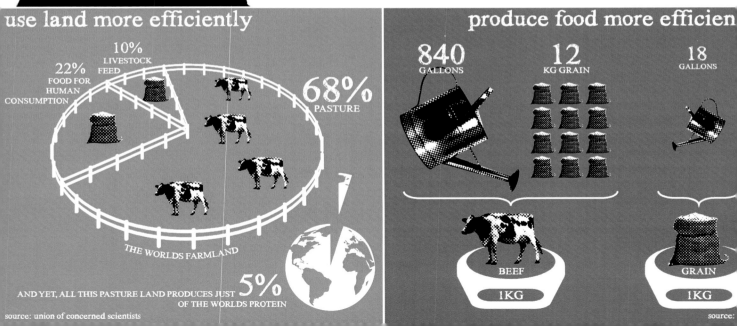

use land more efficiently

22%
FOOD FOR
HUMAN
CONSUMPTION

10%
LIVESTOCK
FEED

68%
PASTURE

THE WORLDS FARMLAND

AND YET, ALL THIS PASTURE LAND PRODUCES JUST 5% OF THE WORLDS PROTEIN

source: union of concerned scientists

produce food more efficien

840
GALLONS

12
KG GRAIN

18
GALLONS

BEEF

1KG

GRAIN

1KG

source:

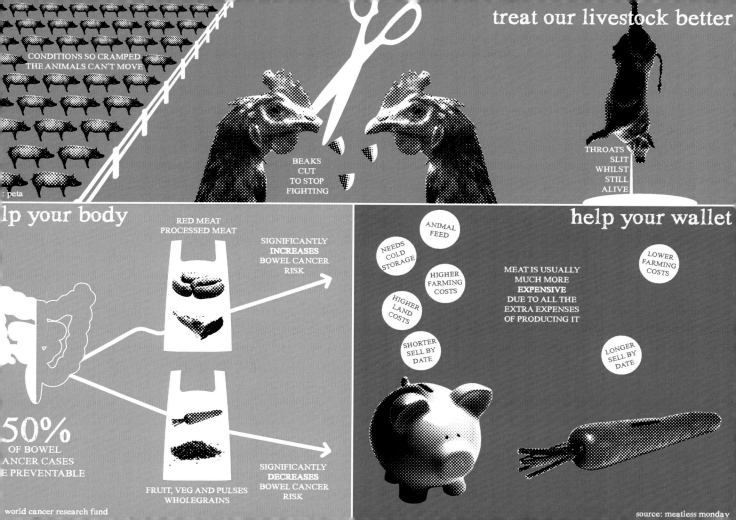

CONDITIONS SO CRAMPED
THE ANIMALS CAN'T MOVE

: peta

treat our livestock better

BEAKS
CUT
TO STOP
FIGHTING

THROATS
SLIT
WHILST
STILL
ALIVE

lp your body

RED MEAT
PROCESSED MEAT

SIGNIFICANTLY
INCREASES
BOWEL CANCER
RISK

FRUIT, VEG AND PULSES
WHOLEGRAINS

SIGNIFICANTLY
DECREASES
BOWEL CANCER
RISK

50%
OF BOWEL
ANCER CASES
E PREVENTABLE

world cancer research fund

help your wallet

ANIMAL
FEED

NEEDS
COLD
STORAGE

HIGHER
FARMING
COSTS

HIGHER
LAND
COSTS

SHORTER
SELL BY
DATE

MEAT IS USUALLY
MUCH MORE
EXPENSIVE
DUE TO ALL THE
EXTRA EXPENSES
OF PRODUCING IT

LOWER
FARMING
COSTS

LONGER
SELL BY
DATE

source: meatless monday

contents

starters/sides

mains

cannellini bean dip with pita chips

A really quick and easy sharer - great as a starter or a snack.

for the dip
3 cloves garlic
a few sprigs of fresh rosemary
1 can cannellini beans (any white beans will also work)
2 tablespoons lemon juice
70ml olive oil
cayenne pepper
salt

for the pita chips
6 pitas
1 teaspoon dried oregano
4 tbsp olive oil

Crush the garlic and lightly fry with most of the olive oil and rosemary for a couple of minutes. Drain and wash the cannellini beans and add to the pan, tossing to coat with oil before tipping into a medium sized bowl.

Add the lemon juice to the bowl and, using a handheld blender, blend the contents into a fairly smooth texture, seasoning with salt and cayenne pepper to taste.

Transfer into a small bowl and top with a sprinkle of cayenne pepper, a little chopped rosemary and a moat of olive oil.

Using scissors cut each pita into triangular wedges and place on a baking tray. Drizzle over the oil and sprinkle on the oregano, then toss to coat and bake for about 10 minutes making sure not to let them burn. Serve alongside the dip.

spiced sweet potato wedges

A favourite amongst family and friends, they go great with salads, pies, quiches, burgers, hummus, in a sandwich - you get the idea!

800g sweet potatoes
3tsp smoked paprika
5tbsp olive oil
flaky sea salt

Preheat the oven to 200°C/fan 180°C/gas 6.

Peel and slice the sweet potatoes into wedges.

Line 2 baking tins with a sheets of greaseproof paper, add the sweet potato, paprika and olive oil, and shake/mix until all the wedges are coated. Bake for 35 - 40minutes, or until golden brown and cooked through, gently flipping the wedges on each tray after about 20 minutes using a spatula.

Serve with a pinch of flaky sea salt.

quick stuffed mushrooms

serves 2-3 as a starter
20 minutes

A really quick, easy and tasty starter.

30g pine nuts
250g whole chestnut mushrooms
160g of cream cheese (at room temperature)
10 - 15 fresh chive leaves
1/4 tsp garlic powder
30ml double cream (at room temperature)
2-3 tbsp olive oil
salt and freshly ground black pepper

Heat a large heavy based frying pan to medium heat, and cook all the pine nuts dry for around 3 minutes or until they start to turn golden brown, stirring regularly to avoid burning. Remove from the pan and leave to cool.

Wash the mushrooms and remove the stems. They should snap off easily where they meet the cap, then finely chop the stems.

Reheat the pan to a medium heat and add the oil. Place the mushroom caps face down, and fry for 3-4 minutes before turning and frying for another 3-4 minutes. Remove from the pan and leave to cool on some kitchen paper to absorb excess oil or water.

Put the cream cheese in a mixing bowl and mix vigorously until the cheese has broken up and resembles a thick cream. Chop the chives and add to the bowl along with the garlic powder, chopped stems, half the pine nuts, and seasoning. Mix well, adding a little of the cream if the mixture is too dry (you do not need to use all of the cream).

Using a teaspoon, spoon the cream cheese mixture into the mushroom caps and sprinkle the remaining pine nuts on top.

roasted tomato soup with pesto croutons

This delicious winter warmer can be served as a starter or a light meal.

for the soup

1.35kg ripe tomatoes
1 tbsp balsamic vinegar
25g fresh basil
1 small leek
3 cloves garlic
1 large potato (about 175g)
2 rounded teaspoons tomato purée
3 tbsp olive oil
salt and freshly ground black pepper

for the croutons

100g ciabatta
2 tsp pesto
1 tbsp olive oil

Preheat the oven to 200°C/fan 180°C/gas 6.

Wash all the tomatoes and slice in half, placing face up on a baking tray. Grind pepper over all the tomatoes then add a few drops of balsamic vinegar on to each. Place the basil leaves in a bowl and mix with 2tbsp olive oil before placing a leaf on each tomato, using the remaining oil to drizzle a few droplets onto each as well. Roast for 40 minutes or until the tomatoes are slightly blackened.

While they roast, chop the leek and crush the garlic. Then fry on a medium heat, together with 1tbsp oil in a large saucepan until the leeks become soft. Meanwhile peel and chop the potato, and when the leeks become ready add the potato along with 500ml of boiling water and the tomato purée, and simmer for 20-25 minutes.

When the potatoes are ready blend until smooth using either a handheld mixer or a blender. Then add the tomatoes and blend a little more, leaving some texture. Return to the saucepan and gently reheat.

Remove the ciabatta crusts, dice into small cubes and toss in a bowl with the olive oil and pesto. Place on a baking tray and bake for 6 minutes. Serve the soup with croutons scattered on top and a little black pepper.

garlic and rosemary focaccia

This easy to make Italian tear-and-share bread is a great accompaniment to any Mediterranean food. You can play around with the toppings too - why not try sun-dried tomatoes, olives, chopped red onions or a range of cheeses?

1 kg strong white bread flour
625ml water (at room temperature so you might want to add a little boiling water to some tap water)
3 x 7g sachets dried yeast
2tbsp white granulated sugar
1 bulb garlic
a few sprigs of fresh rosemary
2tbsp olive oil
salt and freshly ground black pepper

On a clean surface, pour all the flour into a pile, and make a well in the centre. Then pour 300ml of water into the well, and sprinkle the yeast, sugar, and 2tsp of salt on top.

Using a spoon, tip in some of the flour from the edges and mix until it forms a porridge like consistency. Then add the rest of the water and flour, and mix until it becomes a smooth dough. Then, using a little extra flour, dust the worktop and your hands and knead the dough for about 5 minutes, pushing and stretching it around with your hands. Place in a floured bowl and cover with a damp tea towel, then leave in a warm place to rise for an hour.

Tip the dough out onto a floured surface and knock the air out of it, kneading it until for another 5 minutes. Then, grease a fairly shallow large baking tin (around 25x30cm) with oil, sprinkle with a little flour, and spread the dough inside the tin.

Chop off the bottoms of the garlic cloves then, leaving the skin on, crush with the back of the knife and put in a bowl with the rosemary leaves and olive oil press with the back of a spoon to allow their juices to mix with the oil. Pick out the cloves and rosemary leaves with your fingers and press into the top of the bread, twisting each piece in to give the focaccia its distinctive surface texture. Then drizzle ove the oil and leave to prove for another hour before baking for 20-25 minutes at 220°C/fan 200°C/gas 7 until golden.

baba ganoush

An amazing smoked aubergine dip, serve with carrot sticks, cucumber sticks, sliced pepper, the pita chips shown on page 8 or anything else you fancy!

3 aubergines
2 cloves garlic
2 tbsp tahini (a sesame sauce that can be found near the peanut butter or in eastern supermarkets)
1 lemon
a few sprigs of fresh parsley
3 tbsp olive oil

The first stage of this recipe will change depending on what kind of hob or grill you have available:

If using a gas hob
Line the area around the hob with foil as this can get messy. Using a pair of metal tongs hold an aubergine in the flames and keep turning until all of the skin is charred and the shape has collapsed, then repeat with the rest of the aubergines. (You can also do this over a BBQ)

If using an electric hob
Dry fry the aubergines on a medium-high heat in a non-stick pan, regularly turning until all of the skin is charred and the shape has collapsed.

Then slice each aubergine in half and scoop out the flesh, placing it in a sieve over a bowl to allow any excess liquid to drain away.

Meanwhile crush the garlic and mix with the tahini, the juice of the lemon, most of the parsley; chopped, and 1 tbsp of olive oil. Season to taste.

Then mash the aubergine with a fork, or blend gently using a handheld electric mixer, making sure to leave some texture, and stir in the tahini mixture. Pour 2 tbsp of olive oil around the edges of the dish, and top with the remaining parsley.

mango and sesame salad

I came up with this as an ideal accompaniment to a bean burger, the slightly nutty taste of the sesame oil goes beautifully with the sweetness of the mango.

for the salad
a handfull of sesame seeds
1 ripe mango
1 fresh avocado
a few sprigs of fresh coriander
150g fresh greens - spinach, lettuce, mixed greens

for the dressing
2 tbsp maple syrup or honey
juice of 1 lime
3 tbsp sesame oil
freshly ground black pepper

Toast the sesame seeds, either in a pan on a medium heat for 3-5 minutes, or in the oven on an ungreased baking tray for 8-10 minutes, until lightly browned.

Meanwhile chop the mango and avocado into small sticks, roughly chop the coriander and combine with the fresh greens in a large bow

Mix the dressing ingredients in a jug and keep stirring as you drizzle it over the salad to stop the oil from separating. Give the salad a good toss to ensure the leaves have a light coating of the dressing. Sprinkle the sesame seeds on top.

asian pan fried green beans

serves 4-6 as a sid
20 minute

Green beans/string beans/snap beans, whatever you call them this is such a tasty way to cook them. Fried in a Chinese soy based sauce, they've still got that crunch to them and go wonderfully with Chinese food such as fried rice or spring rolls.

500g fresh green beans
2 cloves garlic
3 tbsp soy sauce
1 tbsp balsamic vinegar
1 tsp molasses sugar (if you don't have any, white granulated will work)
1 tbsp sesame oil
2 tbsp peanut or vegetable oil

Fill a large pan with 3cm of water and heat to boiling point. Chop the ends off the beans and boil with a lid on for about 3 minutes before draining and dipping in cold water (this is to keep them crunchy).

Pour the peanut or vegetable oil into the pan and turn to a medium heat. Crush the garlic and add to the oil with the beans, and stir fry for about 4 minutes.

Meanwhile mix the soy sauce, balsamic vinegar, sugar and sesame oil in a small jug and then add to the beans, continuing to stir until th sauce reduces a little. Pour the beans into a serving dish and drizzle the sauce over.

parmesan polenta cakes

These are a perfect accompaniment to Mediterranean dishes such as ratatouille and roasted summer vegetables, but als provide a healthy alternative to potato chips.

a few sprigs of fresh rosemary
35g parmesan cheese
1l vegetable stock
180g instant polenta
25g butter
olive oil
salt and freshly ground black pepper

Line a 20x30cm tin with greaseproof paper, allowing the sides to overhang.

Chop the rosemary and grate the parmesan cheese.

Make up the vegetable stock in a large pan, and bring to the boil over a medium high heat. Slowly add the polenta, whisking constantly to break up any lumps. Continue stirring for a further 5-10 minutes, stirring in the rosemary, parmesan and butter, and season to taste. Spoon out into the prepared pan and smooth out. Refrigerate for 2 hours.

Heat a grill pan to high. Cut the polenta into triangles and brush both sides lightly with oil before placing on the grill pan, cooking for about 3-4 minutes on each side or until golden. You will probably want to do this in batches and keep the cooked cakes warm in the oven.

nutmeg roasted parsnips

Good roast parsnips have to be one of my all time favourite foods! The honey caramelises on the edges adding a beautiful sweetness that complements the festive taste of the nutmeg.

6 medium parsnips
3 tbsp flour
1/2 a nutmeg seed
3 tbsp honey
4 tbsp olive oil
flakey sea salt
freshly ground black pepper

Preheat the oven to 200°C/fan 180°C/gas 6.

Pour the oil into a non-stick roasting tin place in the oven to heat. Peel and cut the parsnips into quarters lengthways, cutting out the slightly woody core, and boil for 5 minutes.

Meanwhile mix the flour with some salt and pepper in a large bowl. When the parsnips are done, drain them and toss them in the flour mixture to coat. Then tip into the hot roasting tin and toss again to coat them in the warm oil. Then leave to roast for 40 minutes or unt⟩ golden.

Grate some nutmeg into the honey and mix well. About 5 minutes before the parsnips are done drizzle the honey mixture over them an⟩ shake to coat before replacing in the oven.

mediterranean pomegranate and feta salad

serves 4 (as a main) or more as a sid
50 minutes (+ 30 minutes cooling tim

This unusual combination of flavours and textures give this dish a delicious tang. A great recipe for summer entertaining, as you can prepare it beforehand and keep it in the fridge.

for the salad
1 red pepper
4 medium aubergines
3 tsp cinnamon
200g green beans
1/2 small red onion
1 pomegranate
200g feta cheese
6 tbsp extra-virgin olive oil

for the dressing
1 garlic clove
1 tbsp lemon juice
2 tbsp balsamic vinegar
5 tbsp extra-virgin olive oil

Preheat the oven to 200°C/fan 180°C/gas 6.

Chop the pepper into medium size chunks, drizzle with oil, and place face down on a sheet of baking paper on a baking tray. Place in th oven for 30 minutes or until the edges start to blacken, then remove from the tray and leave to cool.

Slice the tops of the aubergines and cut into chunks a little larger than a sugar cube, shake over the cinnamon and 1 tbsp of olive oil and roast for 35 minutes, then remove from the tray and leave to cool.

Remove the tops and bottoms of the beans, then bring a large pan of water to the boil with a little salt and cook the beans for 3-4 minutes. When the beans are done they need to be drained and placed immediately in an ice bath (a bowl with some ice cubes and cold water) for a few minutes before draining again and placing in the fridge to keep cool.

Now prepare the fresh ingredients, chop the red onion into thin half moons, cut the pomegranate in half and remove the seeds taking care to not to get any pith, and crumble the feta. Combine these together with the aubergine, beans and pepper. Crush the garlic clove, mix with the other dressing ingredients, and drizzle on top.

roast tomato and parmesan crumble

Both a hearty winter meal but also try chilled with crème fraîche on the side for a great summer dish.

for the filling
500g tomatoes
500g cherry tomatoes
a few sprigs of fresh rosemary
a few sprigs of fresh thyme
1 red onion
20-25 red grapes
1 cup red wine (Merlot if possible)
5-6tbsp olive oil

for the crumble
80g white breadcrumbs
40g grated parmesan cheese
40g pine nuts
salt and freshly ground black pepper

Preheat the oven to 200°C/fan 180°C/gas 6.

Quarter the tomatoes and half the cherry tomatoes and place in a large mixing bowl. Finely chop the rosemary and thyme and add to the mix with 3-4tbsp of olive oil, before tipping out into a large tray and roasting for about 35 minutes.

Chop the red onion into thin half moons and gently fry in 2tbsp oil, until it begins to caramelise. Half the grapes and add to the frying pan along with the wine and simmer gently, adding the tomato mix when its ready, then continue to simmer.

Meanwhile prepare the crumble. If making the breadcrumbs yourself; remove the crusts and cut into chunks before using a food mixer or blender, making sure not to let the pieces get too small. Then mix with the pine nuts, parmesan cheese and seasoning.

Pour the tomato mixture into an oven-proof dish and cover with the crumble mix. Bake for 30 minutes or until a nice golden colour.

broccoli and stilton quiche with walnut pastry

serves 4-
1 hour 20 minute

Tasty hot or cold - the creamy stilton, crunchy broccoli and short walnut pastry provide a wonderful combination of flavours and textures. I've given the quantities for 23cm and 28cm flan tins.

for the pastry

23cm	28cm
50g	75g walnuts
2 tsp	3 tsp caster sugar
150g	225g plain flour
100g	150g cold unsalted butter
salt	

Preheat the oven to 200°C/fan 180°C/gas 6.

for the filling

23cm	28cm
300g	450g broccoli
3 eggs	5 eggs
3tsp	5tsp Tobasco red sauce
200ml	300ml double cream
150g	225g stilton (cheddar if you prefer)
3	5 spring onions

salt and freshly ground pepper

Start by making the pastry. Put the walnuts in a freezer bag and crush with a rolling pin. Sift the flour into a large bowl and add the butter, cutting it into small cubes. Add the ground walnuts, sugar and pinch of salt and rub in with your fingers. Bring the mixture together into a ball and knead for a couple of minutes, then wrap in clingfilm and place in the fridge for half an hour.

Meanwhile cut the broccoli into small heads then boil for 3 minutes before straining, dipping in cold water to cool. Slice the spring onions, then beat the eggs, Tabasco sauce and double cream in a jug, and season.

Lightly grease a fluted, loose bottomed flan tin. Remove the pastry from the fridge and roll out on a floured surface to a size slightly larger than your tin. Using the rolling pin lift the pastry over the tin and gently lift the edges and press into the sides. Cut off any pastry that protrudes more than a couple of centimetres over the sides (you can use this to patch any cracks or gaps). Place a sheet of baking paper inside the tin, fill with baking beans (if you don't have any, rice will do), then bake blind for 15 minutes.

Remove from the oven and carefully slice off any pastry protruding over the edge with a sharp knife. Spread the spring onion and broccoli pieces over the base, crumbling the stilton on top. Pour over the egg mixture and bake for 25-35 minutes until the filling has set

sweet potato and spinach curry

I was always a bit scared of making curries from scratch but this is really easy so don't be afraid! This is a fairly mild curry so great for children or if you aren't a fan of heat, but if you are, just add some dried chilli flakes or extra chilli powder when you add the other spices.

2 red onions
2 green chillies
a 3cm piece of ginger
3 cloves garlic
750g sweet potatoes
400ml can light coconut milk
200g fresh spinach

1tsp ground coriander
1tsp ground cumin
1tsp turmeric
1tsp red chilli powder (2 or 3 if you prefer)
a bunch a fresh coriander
30g flaked almonds
2tbsp olive oil

Finely chop the onions and chillies and grate the ginger and garlic. Fry them together in the olive oil until the onions have softened. The add the spices and fry for a couple more minutes.

Meanwhile scrub the sweet potatoes and cut into chunks leaving the skin on, although you might want to slice off any knobbly bits. The after the spices have been fried, add the coconut milk and sweet potato chunks to the pan and simmer for about 20-25 minutes. You ma want to remove the lid after about 15 minutes to let any excess liquid boil off.

When the potato is soft, chop the spinach very coarsely and add to the pan, replace the lid and cook until the spinach has wilted, then serve and top with some chopped coriander and flaked almonds.

Serve with rice, poppadoms and a healthy dollop of mango chutney.

carrot and goats cheese tart tatin

With little preparation time this simple dish goes well with boiled new potatoes and salad or steamed greens.

6 carrots
50g butter
several large sprigs of thyme
3tbsp runny honey
60g goats cheese (1 small round)
1 roll of ready to use puff pastry
salt and freshly ground black pepper

Preheat the oven to 220°C/fan 200°C/gas 7.

Brush the carrots and slice in half lengthways (no need to cut the tops off). Melt the butter at a medium heat in a large frying pan with most of the thyme and season. Once melted add the carrots, and cook for 15 minutes. Stir every few minutes to ensure the carrots don't stick (if this does start to happen just add a few tablespoons of water).

Line a large rectangular baking tray with greaseproof paper and spread the honey over the paper. When the carrots are finished lay them flat side down on top of the honey making sure they are tightly packed as they will shrink as they cook. Drizzle 2tbsp of the butter and thyme mixture over the carrots.

Crumble the goats cheese over the carrots. Lay the pastry over the tray, making sure all the carrots are covered, tuck in tightly around the edges and cut off any excess pastry. Prick the pastry a few times with a fork and put in the oven for 30 minutes or until golden brown.

Remove from the oven and using a large chopping board, flip the tart and garnish with the remaining thyme.

spicy bean burgers

These burgers go great with either the spiced sweet potato wedges or the mango and sesame salad and also freeze well, so why not make double so there's some in the freezer ready for barbecue time?

for the burgers
2 x 400g cans kidney beans, rinsed and drained
120g bread / 100g ready made crumbs
2tsp mild chilli powder
a few sprigs of fresh coriander
1 egg
3tbsp mango chutney

to serve
a few sprigs of fresh coriander
150ml Greek style yogurt
juice of 1/2 a lime
naan bread (or a gluten-free alternative)
mango chutney
green salad leaves
1/2 red onion

Preheat the grill to a medium-high heat.

Empty the kidney beans into a colander and rinse. Then tip into a mixing bowl and roughly crush using a potato masher, making sure to leave some texture. Add the breadcrumbs (if you are making your own just place the bread in a hot oven for 10-15 minutes and chop in a food processor or blender once cool), chilli powder, chopped coriander, egg, and mango chutney, and mix well.

Split the mixture evenly into 6 pieces and, using your hands, mould each into a burger shape. Grill each side for about 6 minutes or until golden and crisp.

Meanwhile chop the coriander for the topping and mix with the yoghurt and lime juice.

To serve, cut the naan bread into pieces to make the top and bottom of each burger bun. Add a few slices of red onion and some salad leaves and place the burger on top with a healthy spoonful of yoghurt mixture topped with some mango chutney.

carrot & coriander rösti

This delicious dish is great for a light meal, or serve as a vitamin rich alternative to potato chips.

for the rösti
8 medium carrots
4 large eggs
40g chickpea flour
1 large handful fresh coriander
olive oil
salt and freshly ground black pepper

to serve
250g Greek style yogurt
salt and freshly ground black pepper
100g rocket
1tbsp olive oil
1tbsp fresh lemon juice

Peel the carrots and coarsely grate. Beat the eggs in a large bowl and add the carrot, chickpea flour, chopped coriander and a little salt an
pepper. Mix well.

Heat a little oil in a shallow frying pan (preferably non-stick). Take a small handful of the mixture and form into a burger like shape, and
fry until crispy on both sides. Repeat with the rest of the mixture keeping the cooked rösti warm in the oven. If the rösti mixture is not
holding together in the pan, add a little more chickpea flour.

Meanwhile toss the rocket with the lemon juice and oil and season the yoghurt with the salt and pepper.

Serve the rösti warm with a large dollop of the yoghurt on top and the salad to the side.

spanish tortilla with peppers and spinach

This variation on the Spanish tortilla is great hot or chilled. The peppers and spinach give a real Mediterranean flavour and colour but why not experiment with other vegetables? Its a great recipe to use up what's left in the fridge!

750g potatoes
1 red onion
3 cloves garlic
2 red peppers
30g black olives
150g spinach
8 large eggs
50ml sunflower oil
salt and freshly ground black pepper

Peel and chop the potatoes into large chunks and boil for 20 minutes. Drain and leave to cool a little before slicing into 5-10mm disks.

Whilst the potatoes are boiling, chop the onion and crush the garlic and fry with a little oil using a non-stick, high sided, lidded frying pan of about 22cm in diameter. Chop the peppers into small chunks, half the olives and add to the pan, continuing to fry for a further 10 minutes. A couple of minutes before it's ready add the spinach to the pan and stir it in as it begins to wilt.

Beat the eggs in a large mixing bowl and season. When both the potatoes and spinach mixture are ready, add to the eggs and mix well.

Fill the pan with about 3mm of oil and bring to a medium-low heat. Pour the potato and egg mixture into the centre of the pan and shape into a tortilla using a spatula then cover. After a few minutes run the spatula around the edges of the pan to prevent sticking. After 5 minutes frying, place a large flat plate over the top of the pan and drain the majority of the oil into a bowl, then continue to fry.

When the base and sides are golden brown, turn the tortilla out upsidedown onto the large flat plate. Return the oil back to the pan and bring up to temperature, gently sliding the tortilla into the pan so the uncooked side faces down. Once again draining the majority of the oil after a few minutes before continuing to fry until the base is golden brown. Turn out onto a plate to serve and cut into slices.

butternut squash and halloumi hot salad

serves
50 minut

Not your usual salad, this hearty autumnal meal contrasts the earthy beetroot and nutty squash with salty halloumi.

1 medium sized butternut squash
4 medium sized cooked beetroot (not pickled)
1 red onion
4 garlic cloves
120g beluga lentils
1 vegetable stock cube

225g halloumi (1 standard pack)
coriander
2tbsp clear honey
olive oil
salt and freshly ground black pepper

Preheat the oven to 200°C/fan 180°C/gas 6.

Cut the butternut squash in half and scoop out the seeds, separating them from the orange flesh, as you will need them later. Continue to chop the squash lengthways into 8 pieces. Place these on a baking tray with a little olive oil and roast for about 30-35 minutes. Peel the onion and garlic cloves and slice the onion into 8. After about 12 minutes of cooking turn the squash and add the onion and garlic.

Cut each beetroot into 4 pieces. Mix with the honey and 2tbsp of olive oil, wrap in tin foil and place on a tin in the oven for 30 minutes.

Meanwhile prepare the lentils. Pour into a sieve and wash under a cold tap whilst stirring, until the water runs clean. Place in a pan and add 250ml of boiling water, the stock cube, and a pinch of salt and simmer for 25 minutes, adding a little more water if necessary.

Cut the halloumi in half lengthways and cut each strip into slices. When the butternut squash has about 10-15 minutes to go add the halloumi and squash seeds drizzled with a little extra oil.

To serve, unwrap the beetroot and mix with the squash, onion, garlic, halloumi, seeds and lentils in a large bowl, garnish with chopped coriander, and eat whilst warm.

ratatouille

This traditional Mediterranean vegetable stew is summer in a dish. It goes great with polenta cakes, and it keeps well too, tasting even better the next day!

2 courgettes
2 large onions
4 cloves garlic
2 aubergines
2 large red bell peppers
4 tomatoes / 400g tin
a few sprigs of fresh oregano (2tsp dried if necessary)
a few springs of fresh thyme (2tsp dried if necessary)
olive oil
salt and freshly ground black pepper

Preheat the oven to 180°C/fan 160°C/gas 4.

Slice the courgettes into disks and stew in 1-2tbsp of oil, in a covered frying pan on a medium heat, until golden.

Meanwhile slice the onions into strips, and place in a large ovenproof casserole pan. Add 1-2tbsp of oil, cover and put on the hob at a medium heat. Allow to stew gently until soft, adding the garlic, crushed, after a few minutes. The aim is to stew each of the ingredients the oil, not to sauté them. Regularly stir both pans to prevent either from sticking.

While these are cooking cut the aubergines into 2-3cm chunks and the peppers into long pieces. When the onions and courgettes are cooked and golden, add the courgettes to the onions and turn the heat on the casserole pan down a little. Repeat the courgette step with both the aubergine and the peppers, adding them to the casserole pan once cooked.

Once all have been added, roughly chop the tomatoes and herbs and add to the mix, then season to taste. Cover and place in the oven f 45 minutes to allow the flavours to develop. Serve warm or chilled.

50

satay vegetable stir fry

One of the great things about a stir fry is it leaves you free to pick what vegetables you like or need to use up. This simple recipe makes a delicious satay sauce that complements the crisp stir fry vegetables.

for the sauce
150ml creamed coconut
3tbsp sweet chilli sauce
2tbsp soy sauce
3tbsp crunchy peanut butter
1tbsp sesame oil

for the stir fry
300g ready to eat noodles/ 100g dried
1 7-8cm piece of fresh ginger
2 cloves garlic
2 red chilli
a handful of basil leaves
roasted peanuts
3tbsp peanut/vegetable oil

suggested vegetables
1 large carrot
2 red peppers
2 spring onions
4-5 leaves of chinese cabbage
5-6 mini baby corns
50g mange tout
50g bean sprouts

Depending on what vegetables you've bought, thinly chop the carrot, peppers and spring onions and shred the Chinese cabbage.

If using dried noodle nests, add to a pan of boiling water for the required cooking time. If using ready to eat noodles; place in a bowl, pour boiling water over them, and drain.

Meanwhile mix the sauce ingredients in a bowl to make a smooth satay sauce.

Heat the peanut/vegetable oil in a wok. Grate the ginger, press the garlic, and finely chop the chillies and add to the pan. Fry for a minut◌ before adding the harder pieces of stir fry vegetables, such as the carrots and peppers. After a couple of minutes add the noodles and the rest of the vegetables and continue to fry for another couple of minutes.

Move the stir fry to the side of the wok to create a space in the centre. Pour the sauce into this space and bring to the boil before mixing with the stir fry to coat.

Garnish with the basil leaves and roasted peanuts.

breakfast flatbread with avocado and egg

Using avocado as a natural butter, this recipe is a tasty and healthy alternative to the traditional all day breakfast. It's quick too, as the flatbread doesn't use yeast so requires no rising time, and this recipe leaves you with a couple spare for alternative toppings.

for the flatbreads (4)
250g natural yoghurt
250g self raising flour
1 ½ tsp salt
1 ½ tsp baking powder

for the topping (2)
2 large eggs
1 ripe avocado
fresh pea shoots
1 lime
flakey sea salt
red peppercorns (if you don't have these some
freshly ground black pepper will be fine)

Mix all of the flatbread ingredients in a bowl until combined into a smooth dough, you can do this in a food processor if you wish.

Sprinkle a clean surface with a little flour and tip the dough out, kneading it for a couple of minutes to bring it together. Split into 4 pieces and roll them out into thin circular pieces (about the thickness of a pound coin).

Heat a griddle pan or non-stick frying pan to a high heat, and dry fry each piece for a couple of minutes on each side until they go puffy and gain some colour, whilst keeping a close watch not to let them burn.

Add a little oil to the pan and crack the eggs into it, frying on a low-medium heat to your taste. Meanwhile scoop out the insides of the avocado and mash with a fork, spreading out half the puree on the first two flatbreads. When the eggs are ready place one on each flatbread, top with some fresh pea shoots, a sprinkling of red peppercorns, a pinch of salt, and a squeeze of lime juice.

courgette tagliatelle with pesto crumble

This lovely silky summer pasta dish is given a crunch with the addition of a homemade pesto crumble - try with a squeeze of fresh lemon juice if you fancy an extra tang.

for the tagliatelle
3 medium courgettes
1 white onion
2 cloves garlic
300g tagliatelle
150ml crème fraîche
salt and freshly ground black pepper

for the crumble
100g ciabatta
30g pine nuts
1 handful of fresh basil
25g parmesan

Preheat the oven to 200°C/fan 180°C/gas 6.

Slice the ciabatta into chunks and place in the oven for about 8 minutes. Place the pine nuts in a tray and bake for about 3-5 minutes or until a light golden brown and leave both to cool.

Chop the ends of each courgette and grate using the largest holes on your cheesegrater. Finely chop the onion and crush the garlic and fry together with the courgette for about 10 -15 minutes, a lot of moisture will boil off.

Boil the tagliatelle for about 10 minutes with a little olive oil to prevent sticking. When cooked, drain and add to the courgette mixture along with the crème fraîche and seasoning and remove from the heat.

Place the ciabatta into a food processor or blender and blitz for a few seconds to make large breadcrumbs, then grate the parmesan and add this, the pine nuts and the basil to the breadcrumbs and blitz for another couple of seconds until these are mixed in too.

To serve top a large portion of the tagliatelle with a generous sprinkling of the crumble.

winter sage and cheese souffle

The sage and onion stuffing base is the perfect compliment to the light cheese souffle. Serve with nutmeg and honey roasted parsnips for a great festive alternative.

for the stuffing
40g butter
250g onions
a few sprigs of fresh sage
a few sprigs of fresh parsley
75g white breadcrumbs
salt and freshly ground black pepper

for the souffle
110g grated cheddar cheese
40g butter
1tbsp plain flour
500ml milk
5 large eggs
a few sprigs of fresh sage
salt and freshly ground pepper

Preheat the oven to 200°C/fan 180°C/gas 6.

Start by making the stuffing: slowly melt the butter in a small saucepan, finely chop the onions and add them to the pan. Fry for 5-10 minutes or until they're transparent. Chop the sage and parsley and add to the pan along with the breadcrumbs, season and mix well. Remove the mixture from the heat and split into 4 souffle dishes, pressing the mixture gently down in each with the back of a spoon.

Now for the souffle: start by separating the eggs, discarding 1 yolk as we only need 4, placing the whites in a large mixing bowl and the yolks in a smaller bowl. Whisk the yolks with a fork and set them aside for later. Melt the butter in a heavy based saucepan on a medium-low heat, add the tablespoon of flour and mix in well, until it forms a smooth paste. Gradually add the milk, starting with a few tablespoons at a time and continuously stirring to ensure a smooth mixture. Once all the milk is added, keep slowly stirring for a further 7-8 minutes so the sauce thickens. Grate the cheese and add to the pan with the whisked yolks, and stir into the mixture. Remove from the heat, chop the sage, add to the pan and season.

Whisk the egg whites, ideally with an electric whisk, until they're light, fluffy and form stiff peaks when you lift the whisk. Add half the whites to the pan and gently stir in, trying not to knock the air out of the mixture. Add the remaining whites and repeat. Spoon the mixture into the tops of the souffle dishes and mark a circle about a centimetre from the edge with a palette knife to help the top rise. Place in a glass fronted oven if possible to allow you to monitor them and cook for about 20 - 25 minutes.

stuffed peppers with cous cous

This super quick and easy meal is as tasty cold the next day for lunch as it is for dinner so why not make extra? You can experiment too - try substituting in fried courgette chunks, cherry tomatoes, mozzarella cheese and a squeeze of lemon juice for an alternative filling.

2 large red bell peppers
100g cous cous
60g sun dried tomatoes + 1 tbsp oil from the jar
60g olives
60g feta cheese
30g walnuts
a few sprigs of fresh basil

Preheat the oven to 200°C/fan 180°C/gas 6.

Slice the peppers in half lengthways and remove the seeds and white flesh. Brush with a little oil, place in an ovenproof dish and put in the oven for 10 minutes.

Meanwhile chop the basil and place in a bowl with the oil and cous cous, and pour in 150ml of boiling water. Stir and leave for 5 minutes or until all the water is absorbed.

Chop the sun dried tomatoes, walnuts and feta, and half the olives, then add to the cous cous mixture, mixing well to break up the cous cous and ensure an even distribution.

Spoon the mixture into the pepper halves and bake for a further 10-12 minutes.

conversions

1 teaspoon (tsp) = 5 ml
1 tablespoon (tbsp) = 3 tsp = 15 ml
100 millilitres = 0.175 pints
100 grams = 3.5 ounces